The Secret

Art & Healing from Sexual Abuse

Written and illustrated by Francie Lyshak-Stelzer

Safer Society Press
PO BOX 340 • BRANDON • VT 05733

The Secret: Art & Healing from Sexual Abuse

Copyright © 1999 Francie Lyshak-Stelzer

The text and many of the art works were previously published in a different form as an artist's limited edition art show catalog in 1993, copyrighted 1995.

Book & Cover Design: Lindy Gifford, Belfast, ME
Editor: Euan Bear
Production Editor: Jenna Dixon, Bookbuilder, Enfield, NH
Print Coordinator: Wendy Pratt, Rochester, VT
Printing: R.R. Donnelly & Sons

ISBN 1–884444–56–3

$20.00

Order from:

Safer Society Press

P.O. Box 340
Brandon, VT 05733
802-247-3132

Phone orders welcome with Visa or Mastercard.

Library of Congress Cataloging-in-Publication Data
    Lyshak-Stelzer, Francie, 1948–
        The secret : art and healing from sexual abuse / written and illustrated by Francie
    Lyshak-Stelzer.
            p.   cm.
        ISBN 1-884444-56-3 (alk. paper)
        1. Adult child sexual abuse victims—Rehabilitation. 2. Adult child sexual abuse
    victims in art. 3. Art therapy. I. Title.
    RC569.5.A28L97   1999
    616.85'83690651—dc21   99-20781

08 07 06 05 04 03 02 01 00 99   10 9 8 7 6 5 4 3 2 1   1st Printing 1999

This book is dedicated to my readers who are survivors of childhood sexual trauma. My helpers made it possible: Leah Mansbeck, Marilyn White, Richard Morrison, Larry Mitchell, my husband, mother and siblings. To them I owe deep thanks for their help in reclaiming my life.

Preface

Throughout my adult life I have painted. I have painted compulsively, my imagery guided by a voice deep inside. I have always made images about my deepest feelings. My brush and my canvas functioned like an actor on a stage depicting scenes of my inner life. As I wandered through the netherworld of my subconscious, I documented my path with my descriptive images. Without planning to, I created a map of my recovery from childhood trauma.

My journey progressed from blind advance to blinding revelation. Each new discovery produced a wave of shock, fear and rage that later collapsed into grief. As I moved forward in my search, I moved backward through time. I also began making peace with my history and the people who took part in it. In the end, all the pieces of my shattered past were reassembled like a puzzle and the final clarifying facts were revealed. *The Secret: Art and Healing from Sexual Abuse* is the record of my journey, pictures of my inner life, captioned and arranged in an album.

Throughout this process I have worked as an art therapist at a children's psychiatric hospital. I encourage traumatized youth to make art about their own history and needs. I have learned from first hand experience that recovery from trauma is a prolonged process with a natural progression that can all too easily be stifled. Fortunately it can also be encouraged but should never be hurried.

My art studio is my sanctuary—a place of unconditional self-acceptance, freedom and safety from harm. Likewise I create a sanctuary for my young clients in the art therapy room at the hospital. My primary purpose is to create a place of safety—an environment where abuse in any form is not tolerated. Many people who have been traumatized are defeated daily by merciless self-negating thoughts caused by their emotional pain. When these destructive internal self-attacks block the natural creative flow inherent in each of us, my role as an art therapist is to act as a counterforce. The act of making art can be a balm to a wounded psyche. Within the safe environment of the art therapy room, my clients can interact with materials, imagery and language to release the intrinsic reparative potential of their own intuitive acts of self-expression.

For each individual, the artistic process is unique and merits profound respect. During my own treatment, my therapist remained neutral in the face of my emerging memories. It was my place alone to interpret the meaning of my intrusive memories, nightmares and flashbacks. Rather than lead my clients, I affirm them in their self-determined goals. I ask my clients to build a relationship with their imagery and artwork, as if the art produced were their child. I encourage them to respond to their artwork and imagery in ways that demonstrate care, focused attention and an accepting, uncritical mind. The relationship between my clients and their artwork is a mirror of their relationship with themselves. My work is to help my clients establish, recognize and be guided by that relationship.

My work as an artist and an art therapist, my own psychotherapy and recovery from substance abuse all created undercurrents that joined and produced an inner wellspring. It was this wellspring that moved my traumatic memories out of the depths of repression. Image after image surfaced in my conscious mind until I felt compelled to take action. When I was 42 years old I began to take action by talking with my mother about my concerns. When we finished talking I walked out of the house, went to the nearest bar and had the last drink I hope ever to have. Then I walked outside, sat down on a park bench and tried to deal with my shock. I had told my mother that I suspected I had been sexually molested as a child. I was being haunted by peculiar dreams that described the molestation and contained clear fragments of architectural details of the house in which it occurred. I thought that if I could find their actual location, I would discover the identity of my molester. Initially my mother was skeptical. Then she recalled that a neighbor, a few doors down the street, had gone to jail for molesting his daughter when I was 5 years old. Later in the conversation she remembered that I had gone there to play under his supervision.

My sister made arrangements for us to visit the home where my suspected molester had lived. I will never forget the eerie flashbacks I experienced that day, as different locations and interior details that precisely duplicated those from my dream fragments seemed to explode out of scale before my eyes. The memories preserved in my childhood were violently unleashed, unreeling in full sense-surround now that I had arrived at their place of origin. Later on my siblings came forward with their own childhood memories that substantiated mine. I finally had to accept that all my nightmares and painful intimate relationships were actually messages about my own buried history.

When I was exploited and betrayed as a child, my innocence and ability to trust became interlocked with this experience, then the memory was suppressed. Long afterwards, I was haunted by forces born of this toxic episode. My present was perpetually corrupted by my poisoned past as my life slowly turned into a wasteland. In order to save my future, I had to descend underground and excavate what was long buried yet still alive, wounded and festering.

Emotional survival fueled my search. No one ventures into this underworld unless he or she must. None of us dares explore its nether regions without helpers. For those who must set forth on this painful path of exploration and for their allies, this account is a story-map of one possible route. It describes a subterranean passageway where hope seems to disappear. Its most important message to all travellers is that at the end of this tunnel is life-giving light and a worthy destination. By daring to travel this path, a lost self can be retrieved and a prison of death and darkness can be escaped. The treasure to be gained is a wholeness that becomes the seed of a new, healthier, more consciously chosen life.

387184

| DATE | | | | | 19 | | |

NAME

ADDRESS

BARNES & NOBLE #2524
333 NORTH MAIN STREET
WEST HARTFORD, CT 06117

ORDER NUMBER

CITY

STATE   ZIP

OLD BY	CASH	C.O.D.	CHARGE	ON ACCT.	MDSE. RETD.	PAID OUT

QUAN.	DESCRIPTION	PRICE	AMOUNT
	1884444563		2000
			120
			2120
RECEIVED BY		TAX	
		TOTAL	

M 2-4705 REV

The Secret

Art & Healing from Sexual Abuse

Once there was a child. Her mother was always busy with the new baby. Her father was always away.

She was lonely. She took a walk down the road. When the neighbor invited her to play, she was glad. When he held her too close in his lap she was quiet. She had learned at home never to argue with adults.

At nighttime her mother bathed her. She tried to tell her mother about the neighbor and what he did, but she didn't have the words. So her mother didn't understand.

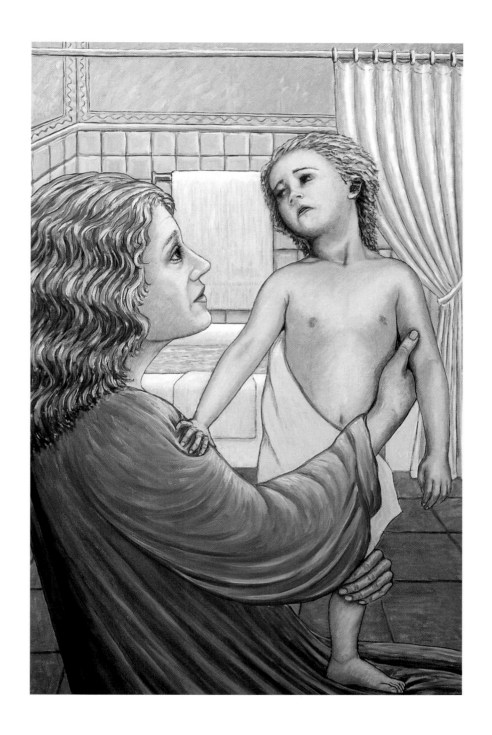

When she saw the neighbor again, he took her into his house. He touched her private parts. Then he told her to keep it a secret, or she would be punished.

For a long time she was a prisoner of the secret. Then, after a while she forgot it.

17

She felt lonely and different from others.
She didn't want to be close to anyone.

When she slept, she had nightmares.
She dreamt she was a doe at the foot of a
volcano. A vulture was swooping down
to capture her for his food.

She dreamt that she was burning alive,
chained to a boat in the middle of the sea.

As she grew older, she was sad and no
longer went exploring.

When she loved, she felt trapped and
powerless and consumed.

Again and again she found herself surrounded
by danger, always playing the fool.

Finally, when the danger threatened to kill her, she fled to the sea. She threw herself into the waters, and was carried to the place of remembering.

As she remembered the secret, her world was blown apart. She remembered her innocence and saw how it had been broken and thrown away.

In time she grew more angry than hurt. And for a long time she raged, until the stored-up anger was spent.

Once the anger had passed, her fear subsided and her dreams changed. The Phantom that before had haunted her, now lifts her out of the sea—an innocent child again.

She dreams that she is nurtured by beasts
instead of consumed by them.

She dreams she swims effortlessly,
carried by the current of a quiet river.

And she dreams of trusting again.

Paintings

About the Author

Francie Lyshak-Stelzer was born in 1948 in Detroit, Michigan. She studied painting and art therapy at the University of Michigan, Wayne State University, and Pratt Institute, earning a masters degree in professional studies. In 1976, she moved to New York City, where she has painted and exhibited her artwork ever since. She is a Registered, Board Certified Art Therapist and Certified Group Psychotherapist at a children's psychiatric hospital in the Bronx. She currently lives in the East Village.

Safer Society Press / Select Publications

Roadmaps to Recovery: A Guided Workbook for Young People in Treatment by Timothy J. Kahn (1999). $18.

The Secret: Art & Healing from Sexual Abuse by Francie Lyshak-Stelzer (1999). $20.

Outside Looking In: When Someone You Love Is in Therapy by Patrice Moulton and Lin Harper (1999). $20.

Web of Meaning: A Developmental-Contextual Approach in Sexual Abuse Treatment by Gail Ryan and Associates (1999). $22.

Feeling Good Again by Burt Wasserman (1999). A treatment workbook for boys and girls ages 6 and up who have been sexually abused. $18.

Feeling Good Again Parents & Therapists Guide by Burt Wasserman (1999). $8.

When You Don't Know Who to Call: A Consumer's Guide to Selecting Mental Health Care by Nancy Schaufele & Donna Kennedy (1998). $15.

Tell It Like It Is: A Resource for Youth in Treatment by Alice Tallmadge with Galyn Forster (1998). $15.

Shining Through: Pulling It Together After Sexual Abuse (Second Edition) by Mindy Loiselle & Leslie Bailey Wright (1997). $14. A workbook for girls ages 10 and up.

Back on Track: Boys Dealing with Sexual Abuse by Leslie Bailey Wright & Mindy Loiselle (1997). $14. A workbook for boys ages 10 and up. Foreword by David Calof.

A Primer on the Complexities of Traumatic Memories of Childhood Sexual Abuse: A Psychobiological Approach by Fay Honey Knopp & Anna Rose Benson (1997). $25.

The Last Secret: Daughters Sexually Abused by Mothers by Bobbie Rosencrans (1997). $20.

37-to-One: Living as an Integrated Multiple by Phoenix J. Hocking (1996). $12.

The Brother/Sister Hurt: Recognizing the Effects of Sibling Abuse by Vernon Wiehe, Ph.D. (1996). $10.

Adults Molested as Children: A Survivor's Manual for Women and Men by Euan Bear with Peter Dimock (1998, 4th printing). $12.95.

Family Fallout: A Handbook for Families of Adult Abuse Survivors by Dorothy Beaulieu Landry, M.Ed. (1991). $12.95.

Embodying Healing: Integrating Bodywork and Psychotherapy in Recovery from childhood Sexual Abuse by Robert J. Timms, Ph.D., and Patrick Conners, C.M.T (1992). $15.

The Safer Society Press is part of The Safer Society Foundation, Inc., a 501(c)3 nonprofit national agency dedicated to the prevention and treatment of sexual abuse. We publish additional books, audiocassettes, and training videos related to the treatment of sexual abuse. To receive a catalog of our complete listings, please check the box on the order form (next page) and mail it to the address listed or call us at (802) 247-3132. For more information on the Safer Society Foundation, Inc., visit our website at http://www.safersociety.org.

ORDER FORM

Date:_____

All books shipped via United Parcel Service. Please include a street location for shipping as we cannot ship to a Post Office address.

SHIPPING ADDRESS:

Name and/or Agency _____

Street Address (no PO boxes) _____

City _____ State _____ Zip_____

BILLING ADDRESS (if different from shipping address):

Address _____

City _____ State _____ Zip_____

Daytime phone (____)_____ P.O.#_____

Visa or MasterCard # _____ Exp. Date _____

Signature (for credit card order) _____

☐ Please send me a catalog.   ☐ Do not add me to your mailing list.

QTY	TITLE	UNIT PRICE	TOTAL COST

SUBTOTAL	
VT RESIDENTS ADD SALES TAX	
SHIPPING (SEE BELOW)	
TOTAL	

No returns.
All prices subject to change without notice.

Bulk discounts available, please inquire.
All orders must be prepaid.

Make checks payable to:
SAFER SOCIETY PRESS

Mail to:

Shipping and Handling

1–5 items	$5	16–20 items	$20
6–10 items	$10	21–25 items	$25
11–15 items	$15	26–30 items	$30
	31+ items $35		
	call for quote on rush orders		

Safer Society Press
PO BOX 340 • BRANDON • VT • 05733

Phone orders accepted with MasterCard or Visa.
Call (802) 247-3132.